Book

of

Din

Book of Din

ISBN: 978-1-948553-04-9

Library of Congress Control Number: 2019931049

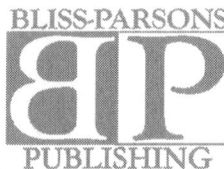

BLISS-PARSONS
BP
PUBLISHING

This book is dedicated to
God

Contents

Entry 1

IN THE BEGINNING

In the beginning there was nothing. Absolutely nothing. That nothing was a total state of PURITY and PERFECTION. Every THING, from the smallest atoms, electrons and quarks to the largest of elephants and whales and mountains and trees, is sentient. Every THING has sentience. And because in the beginning there was NOTHING—no THING within the nothing—the NOTHING itself became the only THING there was. Therefore NOTHING held the entirety of all SENTIENCE in the universe before consciousness was placed within all of the THINGS that would be created in time.

Creation began because of one thought in the mind of God, *God* being the name for the sentient ORIGIN of all things.

WHERE DID GOD COME FROM?

God ALWAYS WAS. God did not come from any THING.

God was the entirety of the nothing that was the whole universe of noTHINGness BEFORE the beginning.

There never really WAS a beginning; God simply always WAS. Just as NOTHING had no beginning, God never began. Creation began at the moment of the release of one thought from the mind of God. One thought—which is a THING—was released by the noThingness of the THING that is God into the void of the noTHINGness that was the universe. Since thoughts are things of mass, the noTHING thought of God became a THING of mass and substance when it reacted with the noTHINGness of the space of the noTHINGness of the universe, and THAT began the process of Creation. The word, *Creation,* does not refer to a Big Bang. That never happened. It refers to the release of the one thought from the mind of God, and the exact moment when that thought became mass and substance upon reaction with noThing.

What was that thought from the mind of God?

It was a single Image of the known universe produced in the mind of God. Even though the universe was nothing and did not yet exist, every atom comprising every planet, constellation, galaxy, star, was known to the sentient mind of God because the nothingness of God was the entirety of Everything, since the Nothing was the Only thing. God brought forth the entire universe with one single thought, just as a photo is formed from a negative. The negative was within the nothing mind of God. He thought it, and the photo developed instantaneously into the universe you see today. Creation is merely the reaction produced by the very first image-thought from the mind of God—the first thing in the noThingness that made the noThing a Thing.

God has total awareness of all universes because they are God's Thought, not the thought of a human. In that beginning Creation Moment, the entire universe was in a state of Purity and Perfection. At a later moment, God Thought beings upon other worlds, then on a whim allowed them to be transported here to thrive on this planet secondarily. But since the first humans on Earth were not a part of the original Pure Thought of God they eventually distorted His Thought, and over time the human culture became like a cancer to the Sanctity of the rest of Creation as they developed. As cancer spreads, so has humanity spread upon this world. The chaotic and impure state of humanity today—its politics, its entertainments, and its religions—are evidence and witness to the impure state of the human species. Now that Earth humans are reaching a state of technology that will enable them to spread their disease to other worlds, if humanity does not return to the SANCTITY of the original state of the universe, God will remove the human disease from this world so that it will not corrupt the SANCTITY of the rest of Creation. Earth will be cleansed so that plant and animal life may continue to thrive on their own in a state of purity and innocence.

Purity and Sanctity are not found within a race or a religion. Humans can only become as they were in the beginning—and save their existence—by cleansing their culture of its contrived impurities and returning to the original THOUGHT of God. It is highly unlikely they will do that.

Entries 2–105
OBSERVATION, LESSONS, AND INSIGHTS

2

GOD is the name humans have given to the SOURCE of the ORIGIN of all things. Although no human knows the true name of God, *God* is acceptable, and should be used in place of common names as it was designed specifically for the purpose of identifying the CREATOR.

3

God and Nature are inseparable. Humans, too, were meant to be joined with Nature and, therefore, to God. That is not working out.

You may have been raised in any one of the myriad Earth religions, but you are uneasy with all the added doctrines, rituals, and man-made opinions that your faith has been encumbered with to the point that you now question everything you have believed all your life. You have felt for a long time that there is something not right in your religion, and in every other religion now practiced on Earth. You can no longer believe that all of the complications, demands and restrictions placed upon your faith should be a part of a practice that you feel in your heart should be a simpler way, a kinder path, a gentler inner knowing—that should be more important than an outward show of gaudy costumes, meaningless traditions, and insignificant ceremony. You long for silence and peace within your heart—you KNOW that is how it truly should be, because you sense deep within yourself that what you find today is NOT the way it was meant to be. What do you do?

4

God does not *require* praise or worship, but if they feel the need, the ONLY religious practices that humans can possibly engage in are genuine and pure offers of praise to God, and the expression of gratitude in their daily lives for all of the gifts God has given to them, especially for the gift of NATURE. Praise and Thanks are the foundation of the TRUE religion that was left here on Earth with the First Beings. These two simple components have been complicated and distorted over the centuries to the extent that the original religion is no longer recognizable.

5

There are two major forces in the universe: God and Mother Nature. God is the sentient Creator of everything, and Mother Nature — created by God — is the sentient energy force that sustains the life of the creation. When God brought all things into existence via the ONE THOUGHT, Mother Nature was brought into being at the same moment.

6

Everything in existence is made up of energy and light—electricity and frequencies with wavelengths shorter than the distance across an atom to those that span the Universe; THAT is a matter of physics. Even YOU are stimulated and controlled by the energy frequencies that are continuously washing over and through you.

That being said, ALL frequencies ORIGINATE with and radiate from God. Imagine a spider web with God at the center. The little threads of the web are all of the energy frequencies used to bring life to all things and to sustain that life. The enormous CREATION FREQUENCY streaming down upon Earth from the vast space that is the Cosmos, is just one of the countless TRILLIONS of threads operating in all the universes.

The Creation Frequency for Earth is the primary Frequency that produces all life on this world. A multitude of secondary frequencies emanate from it to regulate all of the minutiae of all forms of life. If any frequency is disturbed or distorted in any way, then that frequency cannot function properly. For instance, when the frequencies in the human brain that operate the synaptic responses are distorted, damage can and will occur to your brain; your mind can be distorted, and you can die. The same thing is true for the electrical currents of the human heart.

So on a larger scale, when the immense and highly complex Creation Frequency is distorted what do you think the result will be for this world? Earthquakes, floods, volcanoes, tornadoes, hurricanes, fires, droughts—and humans are causing more and more distortion every day. These disasters are not caused by global warming; climate change is simply one of the natural rhythms of the life of this Earth, like breathing or heartbeats. The real damage is caused by billions of human beings producing dark thoughts every day, seven days a week, doing far more harm to the Creation Frequency in one month's time than global warming has in all of Earth's history. It is a matter of physics. Energy effects energy.

7

Regardless of one's religious beliefs, or of one's spiritual path, God does not recognize any philosophies or agendas this tiny world has manufactured for itself, be they racial, sexual, gender, or whatever "pride" one is "proud" of. Political correctness, New Age pondering, and religious denominations are just a few of the many infantile schemes mankind has invented for its fashions and whims with the hope of gaining some sort of power, wealth, or ego-gratification. All of these are meaningless to God. They are fabrications from the minds of mortal Earth humans—they are NOT the Truths of God.

Humans have told other humans that those agendas are important, but that does not make those plans and motives Truth. It makes liars of those humans who, scheming for personal gain, put forth the false agendas. Those who choose to believe the liars rather than the truth are placing themselves on a pedestal equal to or higher than God; for they are attempting to speak for God regarding things of which they have no knowledge. They are attempting to make themselves into gods and goddesses, and that is a very serious and grave mistake.

8

Mother Nature is NOT God, nor is she the Spirit of God. But God, too, is much different from the Creator that human religions here on Earth have come to portray. Humans have distorted the true God into a lesser god of their own manufacture. All power of Creation comes from the Spirit of the true God, and not the god that mankind has invented. When the Spirit of God releases Power into and onto this world, it is released as an energy Force, created by God for the sustenance of that which God has already created and breathed life into. Mother Nature is merely the personified name for that Force.

9

There are no bones that predate the Creation of this Earth, and worlds that have been annihilated leave no remnants behind. They are totally and completely destroyed and dispersed throughout all of deep space as a remnant energy resonance to become a part of what is inaccurately referred to as Dark Matter. Nothing of those sad worlds remains—no planet, no people, no memories. Nothing except for an empty, weak, energy resonance fading away like ripples on a pond.

10

There are Realms into which humans cannot see. There is much preparation going on within those Realms and the time for its revealing is entirely up to God; humans cannot control that. When that time comes, the people of this world will see just how tiny and insignificant they truly are. All of the politics, the petty racial egos, the superficial religions, and anarchistic childishness will come to a swift and terrible end.

11

You are NOT the face You see every morning when You get up and look into the bathroom mirror. You are a Spirit living inside a fragile shell. You live in a shell that You carry around with You. The *You* of You is permanent. The shell of You is temporary. Try to bring that to mind everyday as you journey through this life.

BE AWARE THAT IT IS NOT **YOU** WHO IS WALKING; IT IS **YOUR SHELL** THAT IS WALKING. **YOU** ARE MERELY AN OBSERVER FLOATING FREELY INSIDE THE SHELL.

12

Upon receiving a Higher Truth, one is ready to LIVE the Truth, not just talk about it.

Throughout history, the great religious leaders of this world did not wear suits and ties or cartoonish costumes. They were not accompanied by rock bands or "special music." They did not collect money along the way for their "ministry." They did not start a new denomination everywhere they went. They did not leave lists of rules and pages of laws to be conformed to under penalty of eternal death. They lived for the most part outdoors in Nature, eating wild food, and wearing simple garments; humans can no longer live that way. This world cannot support billion of monks foraging the land for food, but that is only outward behavior, and the outer man is insignificant compared to the inner man.

It is what one practices on the inside and not the outside that counts. True religion is simple, unencumbered and untarnished by the world. It needs no building, no costume, no ritual, no song. It needs only that one acknowledges one's Creator.

13
THE GREAT TREE OF LIFE

The Tree of Life is an analogy for how God's Spirit orchestrates and accomplishes Healing in human bodies and emotions. The trunk of the Tree is the human spine; the branches are the various systems of the human body; the leaves are the product of the functions; the roots are whatever it is the human might base his various, necessary and unnecessary spiritual and physiological beliefs upon. Those roots can either be strong and healthy, or they can be weak and infirm. Strengthen the roots to bring health to the remainder of the tree.

14

Earth Trees sparkle in the wake of an ice storm like diamonds, shining and shimmering with every color in the spectrum like Christmas Trees against the dark grey storm clouds of winter—stunning to look upon, and truly an enchanted sight. The personal aura emitted by each Tree, and the frolicking Tree Spirits leaping about the network of barren Tree limbs in the woods and forests add to the scene, suggesting nothing less than the combined effects of pure magic in a world of supernatural laws of physics and science which has yet to be discovered on this little planet.

15

The majority of planets in this universe do not experience the regular changing of the seasons the way Earth does. There are countless inhabited worlds that are more or less spherical in shape, that rotate faster or slower on their axis—or maybe not at all—making days that are shorter or longer. Other worlds travel around their stars along a path that is longer or shorter, and more circular or elliptical than that of Earth around Sol. There are even some that do not orbit a star at all, but are held in place by the greater forces that surround them in their regions of space. Some planets such as Earth rotate around an axis that is tilted to some degree relative to their stars, resulting in periodic climate changes and variable day/night ratios on the surface of the planet.

All of these variables mean that the passage of time is perceived and measured differently on every single planet in the Universe. In fact, on all other inhabited worlds the measurement of time is irrelevant, for the concept of time, as we know it in our society, does not exist.

16

Humans have personified the forces and workings of Nature ever since humans were first created. God has allowed this out of compassion and as a way of controlling and directing the development of mankind. God knows that all cultures need to develop Truth in small steps, and the naming of the unknown powerful forces at work on this world is merely one of those small steps.

For a long time the names were just fine with God, since assigning names made it easier for a primitive species to presume control and to adapt God's Will to suit themselves while they lived here on Earth. But now it is time for humanity to revive the TRUE concept of God and focus their Worship there, as human-invented worship of the numerous gods and goddesses upon this world has expanded into such a realm of human absurdity that it no longer serves a common good purpose; it now threatens all life.

17

If you are a scientist reading this book, and you wish to be considered a genius, then step out of the box. Throw away the simplistic theories that have been manufactured in haste, fed and kept alive—some for decades—by, arrogance and ego-gratification, or unjust skepticism of new ideas. Bring forth from your own imagination an impossible theory. Perhaps it will, in reality, be TRUTH. Be one of the few brave souls who actually deserves their status, not one of the many scientists out there who are lounging around on bloated, embellished reputations they do not merit, while perpetuating outdated theories that should have been discarded centuries ago.

18

People enamored by this world, it's cultures, it's religions, and its simplistic technology will never find God. God cannot be found when one's mind is buried inside a Smart Phone. God is found in Silence.

When you emotionally interact with the Earth culture in any way, you cease to be the Observer you were meant to be. When you allow the emotions and the activities of other humans to change you, or to bring you down to their level, you cease to be the observer you must be. It is not your duty or your destiny to become like them. You are to be an observer only, so that your principle interaction is with God only. That is the key to life: interaction with God.

19

You can never become God, nor should you wish to. When your physical life ends, if you have honored God in your life, your destiny continues into infinity, and it is a most enjoyable one.

20

What is your purpose in life? Your ultimate purpose is not attained until the next life when you leave the physical and return to your primary form as an Energy Being. You spend this physical life preparing yourself for that purpose. How do you know how to prepare for a purpose if you don't know what that purpose is? If you interact with God in the ways explained in this book, God will guide you so that you will be prepared for your next life exactly as necessary. If you do not interact with God, or if you do not believe in God, you will not have a next life, or a purpose.

21

Who are you? You are a Being of light and energy housed within a limited mortal frame that acts as a vehicle to allow you to move around on this world, throughout your short life while you achieve learning and gain knowledge of your true nature.

22

What is death? Death does not exist. The physical human body eventually ceases to function as an effective vehicle for human transport, but the atoms that make up the human body remain active and become some other thing when the Spirit Being exits the physical body. If a human has succeeded in properly interacting with God during this life, that human's Spirit Being will continue to live into infinity with consciousness and activity. If the human has not properly interacted with God during this life, that human's Spirit Being will be dissipated into the noTHINGness of deep space, without memory, consciousness or activity.

23

It is impossible to enlighten the ignorant of this day regarding certain things they can never understand because their own biases and preconceived ways of seeing has put them out of their reach. Humans today are unable to comprehend that which has always been, and remains to this day; that is, the great Mysteries of God that were never meant to be distorted by the flawed and judgmental thinking promoted by all religions on Earth.

24

Mother Nature is like the beat of the human heart; if the beat stops, the human dies. Without Mother Nature's sustaining resonance, all life everywhere would cease to exist. It would not just merely die, it would evaporate—vanish completely. Even its very memory would cease to be. No recollection whatsoever that LIFE had ever been created or existed in any form on this or any other world would remain.

25

It is time for humans to lift their eyes and look into the deep night sky for the SIGNS that will soon be upon them. Whether the signs bode well for the future or warn of destruction is up to humanity.

26

Many scientists would have you believe that the first human beings simply emerged some time between ten thousand and one million years ago, having evolved gradually from apes, or fish, or birds, or pond amoeba, into rather ape-like, human-like creatures, Australopithecus—you know the most famous of these as Lucy. In reality, the truth of their origin lies within the ancestral memory of many Earth humans, but the constant state of chaos the contemporary human mind is immersed in on a daily basis prevents all but the tiniest glimmer of that memory from breaking through to the conscious or even the subconscious mind.

27

The human beings in Egypt throughout the time of the pharaohs produced a splendid civilization. It defies the laws of science as known at that time, as well as simple common sense and reason, that they could have achieved it all in and of themselves. Well, they did not—they had help.

28

Praxiteles was one of the greatest artists who ever lived on Earth. His statues were so realistic that people passing by one standing outside a temple or in a public place would often greet the statue by saying *Hello*, expecting the statue to return the greeting. Most of his sculptures have disappeared over the centuries. Many of them were taken away by the Romans who redid them a bit—often with the face of an emperor or senator—and who would then take credit for them. Others were simply lost or destroyed with the passing of the ages. Praxiteles was not of this world.

29

What is time? It is not. It is only a word. The concept of time does not exist as a separate entity of space, dimension, or Being. Time is an Earth word that labels increments of existence that are of a concern to human beings on Earth. The concept of Time does not exist on any other world except for Earth. If you were to show a watch or a clock to a Being from another world they would have no idea as to what those items are.

30

Contrary to what you may have heard, the universes are not holographic, and there are no universes existing as 2-D slices while only appearing to be 3-D, as suggested by one of the latest scientific theories.

There is a great deal of speculation among scientists and philosophers regarding how many of the supposed other-dimensional universes might exist. One popular notion suggests that there are eleven, each one operating at a different frequency so they can all exist within or on top of each other without interfering with each other's existence. Where the number, eleven, came from is anyone's guess—maybe because it correlates to the number of dimensions as proposed by another popular theory that is also incorrect.

Three or four, ten or eleven, twenty-six or infinite, the number is irrelevant because there are NO other-dimensional universes—ZERO. All conjectures along that line are incorrect, clichéd, and must cease immediately. Years are passing by, wasted on such frivolity of thought. You will not get off this planet and out of this Solar System until you begin to think as others think on other worlds. Yes, there are many universes, but they are 3-D, just like the one in which you now reside.

31

The poet and artist, William Blake was thought by many to be mad. Most of his contemporaries refused to speak to him or even about him. He was incorrectly called a revolutionary because the other artists believed he was rebelling against the way things had always been in the world of art.

In reality, Blake was not rebelling against anything. He couldn't have cared less about the accepted standards of traditional art, society, religions, or anything else of any import to such a primitive society. He wasn't on Earth to rebel; he was here to introduce the human brain to intricate new ways of thinking. He was here to stimulate the imaginations of those on this world who were not content to wallow in the mire of the ordinary, but who wanted instead to explore the farthest limits of the human mind in order to solve mysteries, answer questions, and convert dreams into reality.

To see the world in a Grain of Sand
And a Heaven in a Wild Flower
Hold Infinity in the palm of your hand
And Eternity in an hour

From "Auguries of Innocence," by William Blake

32

For every atom in every created thing in the larger universe, there lives another entire universe within it.

33

**78,000,000,000,000,000,000 = THE NUMBER OF ATOMS
IN ONE GRAIN OF SAND—GIVE OR TAKE A FEW.**

Consider the fact that every atom exists as a solar system of sorts, not unlike Earth's solar system. This is just an analogy of course; an atom does not perfectly mimic a solar system. A single atom is made up of several components: positively charged protons, negatively charged electrons, and neutrons that have no charge at all. The protons and neutrons are clustered together in the center of the atom in what is called the nucleus. The relatively tiny electrons are found outside the nucleus, buzzing around in orbit. The larger protons and neutrons are themselves made up of smaller particles called quarks and gluons, with the gluons functioning to glue the quarks together.

An atom is similar to a tiny solar system in that all of the little subatomic particles orbit the center of the atom, just as planets orbit around their star.

What is a star? In simple terms, it's a great big ball of energy like the atom's center, which is also a ball of energy. Each and every atom in a single grain of sand resembles to a certain degree a single solar system in your universe out there. So in effect, there are 78,000,000,000,000,000,000—that's 7.8×10^{19}, as they say in scientific circles—little solar systems busily orbiting about inside (making up) ONE single grain of common Earth sand. The entire Milky Way Galaxy contains only about 250 billion—2.5×10^{11}—stars. Or maybe it's only 100 billion. Then again, it could be 400 billion; new stars are being added at a rate faster than a human can count.

So, how many solar systems are contained in all

of the grains of sand on all of the beaches here on Earth alone? More than even a googolplex. A googol is a lot—the number one followed by one hundred zeros: $1\mathrm{x}10^{100}$. A googolplex is simply a one followed by a googol of zeros, or $1\mathrm{x}10^{googol}$.

A googolplex is equal to 10 to the power of googol—that is, 1 followed by 10 to the power of 100 zeros. There are so many, it would be impossible to calculate. Now multiply that by the number of grains of sand on all planets in all of the universes out there, then go outside into your yard, stoop down and scoop up a handful of dirt and sand. You will be holding infinity in the palm of your hand.

34

Life's energy is in constant motion along the continuum that exists between the poles of opposites. A human is never forced to remain stationary in any one spot in the continuum—one day the human may become like an electron, existing in many different places at the same time, whether one is speaking of mental revelations or physical experiences.

35

The Higher Truth that governs everything in this universe must now be taught. It must replace what society has wrongly put in its place. If this Higher Truth is not only taught, but also applied to the world culture, then everything and everyone will run smoothly. Everything and everyone will be in balance and harmony. If not, the world will deteriorate and come to a terrible end, and THAT is the simple secret solution to nearly every problem facing mankind today; the answer to every question.

36

Do NOT start commanding your body to do this or do that because you have been told that you are Divine, and therefore you should be able to command the molecules and cells of your body to heal themselves. You are NOT Divine—only God can be given the title, Divine.

You cannot command anything in your body. You cannot heal anything. Healing comes only from the God Who created you and Who knows how to heal, and from the willingness of the atoms within you to heal you for a specific purpose. Consider seriously what I write; you will not read these Truths anywhere else.

37

The energy produced by a nuclear bomb is forced from the atom by the will of man. How much more energy would be produced if it were not forced from the atom, but the atom gave it up of its own choice?

38

You must begin to think differently if you are to understand the Truth. It is that understanding which will lead you to the ability to do amazing things with your mind, to heal your own body, and to repair your own planet. If you can only understand how the atomic structure of created things works, you will be able to work with the atoms themselves to secure healing for your body. So far, no scientist on Earth has even begun to understand this.

This is not the simple exercise in positive thinking, positive affirmation, or visualization that you may have heard of or even attempted to practice. None of those things have any power. Do not believe the New Age hype. The only way to be the catalyst for healing in your physical body, in your mind, or for your world—your Spirit never needs Healing—is to work in cooperation with the atoms themselves. If you learn WHO the atoms truly are and you befriend them, they will work with you, for they are sentient Beings, and will cooperate with humans—IF the will of the humans is the same as that of the Will of God, which is to bring The Great Plan to fruition.

39

One purpose of this Book is to get you to think outside of the box you have been living in all of your life. You must throw away all of your preconceived notions of how everything in and on this world works and has it's Being.

I use the language of mathematics, science and physics to illustrate my points, but you need to understand that the principles of math, science, and physics as found on this world are so simplistic that any child on most any of the other planets throughout your universe would find discussion of them to be unbearably boring. All of the technological achievements you look to with pride and consider to be so valuable to your own lives, pale in comparison to those of other worlds in your universe, some of which are located very near to your own. In the Alpha Centauri star system, a mere 4.3 light years distance from Earth, there are hundreds of inhabited planets, most of which are far superior in technological development and the ways of God than Earth will ever be.

40

I am meant to take hold of you and shake you into the realization that you are not who you should be at this time in your development. One of my purposes is to offer to you the shortcuts and immediate advantages of a technology that is far beyond your wildest dreams. I cannot do that, though, as long as you continue to wallow in the infantile state you apparently enjoy and seem reluctant to leave behind. I simply do not trust you enough to give you any more than is necessary at this time. I fear that your leaders would acquire the information and use it to achieve their own selfish political goals, for that is the attitude they exhibit with their every breath.

41

Humans are at a fork in the road. One direction is the way to ultimate peace and prosperity, while the other leads to immense pain and ultimate annihilation. The fate of this world is entirely up to the humans that reside upon it. As of this writing, humans are doing very little to change their world for the better, and the time to change is growing short.

42

The most critical need on this planet right now is for all of humanity to detach from ego. This must happen on an individual basis, so as to affect the whole. There is no way around this. There is no collective prayer that will get humanity out of the destiny it has created for itself. Every single person on this planet needs to look first to the stars, and then begin their own release.

43

The power of evil in this world is being enhanced by negative human emotions that have now taken on a life of their own. If this continues, this planet will evolve into a chaotic state the likes of which no human has ever seen before—it has already begun.

44

In order to advance above this world, a person must leave the politics and laws of this world behind. One must graduate to the Higher Laws of God.

45

Every one of the physical universes within the Greater Universe contains solid matter, well-ordered galaxies, constellations, solar systems, stars, and planets, similar to our own universe, U48. Each of these universes is so vast as to seem infinite in its own right, and in a way they are. They exist very close together, almost joining each other, with only a narrow band of empty space separating one universe from another.

It is possible to jump from one universe to another by crossing these bands, or Borders, in a manner similar to the Area Dimensional Jumping that is used by more advanced Beings to travel between the planets and galaxies of U48 in a matter of moments. It is possible to travel to the end of this universe where you will be met with light years of darkness, but if you carry on into the darkness and beyond you will eventually reach the border of another physical universe similar to your own.

46

The only thing that is impossible in this and in all the universes is that which humans believe to be impossible. Nothing is impossible with God. Nothing is set in concrete. God can create, reshape, re-pattern, rearrange, dissipate, dissolve, destroy, reinvent, or totally re-create anything God wants—anytime, anywhere. It is unfortunate that so many who are working in the various sciences do not believe in their Creator, or are even antagonistic to the very concept of a Creator Being—other than themselves, of course. One day they will be shown that their ego-fed, lack of belief, was a terrible mistake. They will pay dearly for that false belief.

47

The ancients could never see God face to face, but they thought they could feel or sense God in all of Nature. To them, rocks and boulders were more than just those big hard objects seen hanging on the sides of cliffs next to state highways. Flowers were more than those colorful little things you mow down in your front yard. Everything in Nature had life, Spirit, and Sentience. Everything still does; humans just can't feel it any more. They do not want to feel it. They love their plastic and metal more than they love God's creations.

48

Leave behind everything you think you know about dimensions. For Earth humans, there are only four Dimensions, and they are not layered upon top of each other. One is the Physical Dimension in which you, the reader, now find yourself. A second dimension acts as a Buffer and Portal between the universes and is used only by the Higher Created Beings. A third dimension coordinates Jumping from planet to planet within this galaxy. A fourth dimension is used by a few other Higher Beings to Jump in and out of human containers—that is, bodies—on Earth, which they have been doing for a very long time. There are a few other created dimensions that are reserved for purposes having little to do with this planet and are operated only by Higher Beings, but you have no reason to be concerned with those, as you will never experience them. It is enough to ponder the dimensions that directly affect you here on your world.

49

Aliens are already here and have been here for eons, but shiny metal ships from other planets simply do not exist and never have existed. If you think about the vast distances between even the closest star systems, you will have to admit that it is impossible for metal ships to travel at the speeds necessary to go from star A to star B before the ship runs out of fuel, falls apart, or is destroyed by meteors, asteroids or other Beings. Even if it were powered by star energy, an inertial force, or perpetual motion, it would take much too long to get from one planet to another and all those aboard would die of old age. No aliens have ever traveled from planet to planet in this manner. It has never happened and it will never happen. It CANNOT happen. If you believe it has or will, you need to pull your mind out of that mental box I wrote about earlier, for you are still thinking in antiquated, quite frankly, unproductive ways.

It is possible to travel from planet to planet throughout this entire universe, but it must be done within the parameters of the Laws of God—not the laws of Earth physics, the Universal Laws, or even the laws of Sci-Fi. Humans must learn to go beyond the tired, worn out concepts that scientists, and even Science Fiction believers, have been tossing around for years. They must truly begin to *boldly go where no one has gone before*, and quit limiting their imaginations. They must stop wasting time on the old metal ship, wormhole, and time warp nonsense. These concepts that have never been more than theories, and like most theories on this world, they are inaccurate and do not work.

50

THE HIGHEST LAW OF ALL

Whatever goes against the Great Plan of God will be removed by God.

51

If you wish to continue to remain in existence You MUST change the way you think and act. There is no argument in this matter, no court of law, no voting about it, no politics or legislation, no self-important politicians, no *I forgot* or *I'm sorry, I wasn't thinking*. There are no excuses—physical, mental or emotional. There is no appeal to self-esteem. No safe rooms. There is only THE CREATOR'S LAW—implemented perfectly in less than a heartbeat throughout this and all other universes.

52

Neither time nor distance is of any concern in space. Time exists nowhere except in the minds of human beings who invented it here on Earth. If one knows what to do, one can travel anywhere in this universe in a matter of moments. A journey of twenty billion light years takes no longer than a journey of 450 light years—all such journeys in outer space take less time than an Earth human takes to walk from one side of the street to the other.

53

Why do bad things happen to good people? The answer is simple. First, there are NO good people on this world. And second, all of the evil and bad that occurs on this world has been invented and allowed to happen by, the people of this world; God has nothing to do with it.

In the beginning, God created a perfect world without disease, evil, or disasters. At that time, humans were good, and did not worry about evil, disease, or disaster. Over time, the selfish decisions made by humans created the disease they now call evil, and through the exercise of the Free Will that God had given them, humanity continued to make bad choices, and evil spread like a plague. The only way to remove evil from this world is for ALL of humanity to return to God—not religion or philosophy, but to God. Treat each other with kindness, and treat the Creation with respect; that is the ONLY medicine that can heal the illness of evil. God's only role in this is to observe how humans react to the bad choices they make. Will they choose to make the sacrificial decisions necessary to correct those bad choices? Those sacrificial decisions, if they are even made, will determine the final eternal destiny of each person on this world.

54

God emanates a Spirit of Harmony into all Creation, therefore it is logical that God would give Earth humans one final chance to change back into the innocent Beings they were when they were Seeded upon this world. It is a shame that the mass ego of the Earth human culture will probably never be able to admit it was wrong. The probability that they will return to God and to the Laws of God and leave behind their infantile abominations is small.

It is sad that the majority of humans on Earth have chosen to serve other gods: to follow popular political and societal/political/racial cult figures instead of their God; those who have done so and who do not change their ways will not be happy in the afterlife—they will not HAVE an afterlife.

God does not consider anyone to be good who remains neutral while evil is carried out around them. There is no such thing as a moderate follower of God. Every neutral and every moderate will be removed from existence in the End.

55

God did not invent religion with its thousands of different denominations and conflicting beliefs—humans did. God did NOT invent the laws we find in religions today—humans did. In the beginning commandments and laws were not necessary. All Beings everywhere inherently knew how to behave and how to interact kindly with each other. There was no crime, no violence. If everyone on Earth loves God, then man-created laws are not necessary. Man-created laws were added later in your history in order to control a situation that should never have happened in the first place – the corruption of humankind through the accumulation of too many bad decisions. In reality, the only Laws of God are:

1. The highest Law: God will remove whatever goes against the Great Plan of God.
2. Humans are to recognize that there is only one Creator God, and to acknowledge that He created the universes—throwing out all other human-invented concepts of gods and goddesses.
3. God is to be Worshiped in private in your daily life, by being thankful for your life and for the creations of Nature around you.

Even today, after thousands of years of subjection to religious laws, human culture is more deviant than ever. What good have laws done? Humans have reached a point of no return; man-made laws will not help them. At this point in your history human behavior is so decadent and self-serving that it is doubtful that humanity can save itself from utter annihilation. The salvation is to be found only by adopting and practicing the above three Laws of God, and doing it before it is too late.

56

Contrary to popular Earth belief, all life is NOT sacred in the grand scheme of things. The caveat is that those Beings who perpetrate abominations to God are not considered worthy of remaining in existence and are terminated. Only those life forms that are in obedience to the Laws of the Creator are considered sacred. They are the life forms that will enter into their own personalized Heaven to reside there eternally. It is unfortunate that Earth humans have chosen to distort God's Laws. As a result, there are few humans at this time who will be allowed to experience the Greater Reward.

57

There are no such things as politics, democracy, religion, race, civil rights, or personal rights, in this or in any other Universe. Those concepts were invented and put forth erroneously by Earth humans. These ideas have been allowed to continue unchecked only on Earth and nowhere else, and they are an embarrassment in the legacy of this world. There is only ONE UNIVERSAL LAW governing ALL of CREATION, and that is the LAW OF THE CREATOR.

58

Every time a conflict occurs, that is, when two opposites come together in the same time and space, the result must be the release of energy that usually brings about the destruction of the opposites. Therein lies the Power. This is the Power of Rejection.

59

The restrictive religious dogma, false social and political beliefs, indifference, and the destructive forces of atheism that are rampant across this planet, have caused the near-total destruction of the attunement of life's interconnectivity. The Creation Frequency is suffering increasing damage and dilution. This must change soon or humanity will not survive. Powerful Beings have been put on call to act on a moment's notice to destroy those who destroy the Creation. Listen to these words in your heart as you read them.

60

REGARDING HUMAN BEHAVIOR

There is a reason the Golden Rule is embedded within the scriptures of nearly every religion on this planet. The Golden Rule, although it was not called that at the time, is the remnant of a principle that was gifted to this world by God during the Seeding of the first Beings on Earth. The rule is a simple one. It states that a human is to *Do unto others as you would have them do unto you*. Common sense really. You don't want them to kill you, so you don't kill them. Violence of any type should not be committed on Earth except in self-defense. Nor should a person harm any other person in any way. Such punishments are left to God and His Higher Beings. This Golden Rule was the only rule for behavior regarding humans toward other humans revealed to Earth. All other rules and commandments came later, after humans corrupted the Earth to the extent where such rules became necessary.

61

God did not invent a list of commandments, man did. God gave us laws of physics and science and common sense behavior, not of moralistic dos and don'ts that change from culture to culture, and from invented religion to invented religion.

The religions of man are NOT from God; God speaks only through His Creation. To describe God, or to put commandments into His mouth, or to demand that a person act this way or that is ludicrous. To claim *this is sin* and *this is not sin*, is not of God, but of man. Sin, which is commonly defined as doing what is wrong in the mind of God, implies that a person KNOWS what is wrong or right in the mind of God. Even human-invented scriptures teach that humans can NEVER know the mind of God, so how is it possible for them to invent rules of sin and non-sin?

God did not invent the clergy, or priesthood, or organizations to act as mediators between God and humans—humans invented them. God did not invent a list of required rituals, a list of proper costumes to wear—humans did. If you wish to perform your own ritual for the worship of God, fine, you may do so, but it should be personal, private, silent, and meant only for your individual life and not others. Worship is only between God and you. To force organized worship onto a human is to take the meaning out of it. Every human will have his or her own private way of worshiping God, and that is fine. It is only when groups of humans get together, invent communal rules for worship, and demand that all others worship their way, and ONLY their way, that problems arise. At that point, worship on Earth becomes void and meaningless.

62

EVIL is a human concept that has never been and can never be accepted by God. This is not something God has created—that would be impossible. The human invention of evil can never truly exist in the Presence of God. What humans perceive as evil is merely an experiment by rebellious human minds that have gone astray over the centuries. The repetition of so-called evil acts among the populace has allowed the energy of evil to accumulate and to become personified as a powerful force for darkness. This force has been given a name by many of your religions, the most familiar of which is satan. Satan is real, in that you have given him power. Ceasing to give him power can destroy him, but it is doubtful that certain segments of humanity will be willing to do that.

63

It should be a matter of simple common sense for everyone to realize that God is a vast Cosmic Intelligence that has only Spirit as substance. It should also be obvious that since God is always in a Spirit Form far different from human beings, then just about everything about God will be a mystery and nearly unfathomable to the human mind.

No human has even a clue as to WHO GOD REALLY IS, much less how God functions, where God came from, or how the process of Creation really works.

64

Humans can personify the myriad energy forces and frequencies governed by God all they want in order to relate to and understand them, but to personify God Himself serves only to belittle and debase the ONE CREATOR. To reduce the ONE CREATOR to the level and scope of human beings, all of whom are tainted by their own evil accumulated over eons through the practice of unspeakable acts of violence and immaturity, is an abomination in the Eyes of God.

Humans need to reconsider the ways they represent their Creator. If they TRULY believe in God and TRULY have faith that God hears their prayers, then wouldn't they want to throw out the false, concepts of worship and devotion invented by humans, and replace them with TRUTH? Wouldn't they wish to abolish false religions, and do ONLY what God asks of them? Wouldn't they wish to stop searching for God inside enclosed buildings of mortar and steel, and return to TRUE Worship of God in the Presence of Trees, Stars, and Running Streams?

65

Most of the religious instruction that was Seeded with the Earth culture years ago centered in and around Nature. Humans were created to be a people of Nature, and bore little resemblance to what they have become today. In those ancient days, humans could communicate with birds and animals. They could learn from the trees and the weather. They could cross over into other realms of Nature by using the mystical bridges—energy transporters of a type left for their use by the First Beings—found throughout the wild areas they lived in. There is no human today who can do these things. Not one.

66

In the beginning, Devotion was a Truth of life. It was an inherent fact within the newly Seeded humans that a Creator God exists, and all humans everywhere just KNEW that the Creator was to be thanked and respected on a daily basis and in all that they did. There were no church buildings, temples, rituals, dogmas, doctrines, meeting times, insipid music, goofy religious costumes, NOTHING. The worship of God, to the original Earth humans, was a daily, personal thing. The most common way that individuals gave thanks to God, or worshiped God, was to go outside in the evening, look up at the night sky, and simply say Thank You.

67

Silly—it is all very silly, but even so, it has become a serious matter of contention and even violence in the current Earth culture. Humans now have thousands of religions and worship millions of different gods and goddesses. The doctrines and dogmas of each religion are so different from each other that each group feels it necessary to fight with all of the other groups about those differences.

Where mankind was once supposedly evolving into a super, advanced race of Beings, today we find only primitive nonsense, war, hatred, infantile racial pride, politics and abominable violence done in the name of this or that god or goddess. Most of the wars and arguments on this planet are actually the result of one religion killing members of another over a difference of opinion regarding the afterlife.

Can you see the irony in that? They are all, literally, dying to protect their opinion about where they go when they die, when in reality, none of the dead can ever come back to deliver the Truth as to whether they were correct or not. It is all beyond absurd. It is an abomination in the eyes of the TRUE CREATOR Who will soon correct the situation, and no one on this planet is going to enjoy that correction.

68

There is so much mystery in this universe—but it's really not mystery, is it? Humans make it all up. In and of itself, the universe knows all about itself; all questions are answered, and there are no mysteries. Humans have manufactured their own empty mysteries, including their own gods that vary in description with every religion on Earth.

Heaven is eternal. Do you really see yourself sitting around in a lotus position contemplating your bliss for endless time? How long do you think you can do that before you tire of the boredom? As all things are created to seek improvement, so are humans. Heaven is a place of advancement and progress, not a place of false contentment for having attained some state of being that requires nothing more than to sit around and doing nothing but feel good about yourself and your situation.

Humans are on this world to learn and to become. Those who do so will return to their own Heaven.

69

In ancient days it was an accepted fact that God was a Mystery. God's ways were irrelevant to the first culture. Everything just happened. Everything just worked. No one even cared to define the Mystery, or start a religion about it. Worship of the Creator could not be separated from anything else a person did. The reverence a person felt for Nature and for the very breath in their lungs was worship, and it was just an everyday thing, as normal as eating food, or enjoying a walk in the forest, or breathing. No one thought anything about it, it just WAS. That is the way it should have been, and that is the way it should be still today. That is the way God wishes for it to be. Later on I will give you simple instructions on HOW to worship God. You can follow the instructions or not; it is your choice. But if you choose to follow them, you must follow them exactly as they are given.

70

The First Beings would be appalled by a contemporary worship service in a church building that contains no REAL worship. They would be appalled by the rituals and silly productions put on by all churches and religions around this world today. The loud productions of music and the entertainment extravaganzas would not be tolerated because their energies and frequencies are destructive and cause serious damage and pain to the Life of Nature around them. The First Beings would shake their heads in disgust at what religion has done to TRUE Worship in the sanctity of the silence of Nature. The ancients were primarily farmers. They cared about crops and rain and rivers and seasons. They were connected with Nature in every facet of their lives, and they saw God as being present in every cell of everything around them. They would not be able to understand how or why the religions now practiced by Earth humans have removed all mention of Nature from their services.

Nearly every one of the parables and deeper teachings found in human scriptures were drawn from Nature. Why have humans removed the POWER of those Teachings? Religious leaders taught nearly every one of their lessons outside in Natural settings, why do humans insist on attending church inside hollow buildings? The First Ones would exclaim:

Where is God in this human-built place? God is not present here! Where is the Mother of Humankind, the Power of all Nature? If she were here, she would tear this building to the ground in one blink of her eye.

71

Millions of years ago, a Spirit of Goodness and Health enveloped this planet. Today, an evil spirit corrupts everything it touches. When Earth was first Seeded, Nature was alive in every Being. All life was related and every Nature Being was to be treated with the same respect that one would show a human being. Life was sacred to every original inhabitant of Earth because the SPARK of energy that sustained the life in all things came directly from God. The Spirit of the tiniest speck of dust was just as valuable as the Spirit of the most noteworthy human being. That spark of energy remained connected to God because it came from God, and if, for instance, the energy of one human was connected to God by some sort of supernatural thread, and the energy of a specific Tree was also connected to God by it's own supernatural thread, then the human and the Tree were also connected to each other in a supernatural way. They were related. They were family. The First Ones understood that.

72

Mother Nature is the Primary representative of the Creator, and carries all aspects of the Creative Energy—both the gentle and the terrible within her. You must never forget that. The creative and the destructive are just two small aspects of Mother Nature's total Being. The decisions that she wills forth are part of her reason for Being, and she will never deviate from TRUTH. Regardless of how humans paint the picture of their man-made gods, Mother will fulfill the instructions of the REAL God to perfection. In the near future, humanity will witness both Mother's compassion and her judgment upon a planet that seems to care more about a physical life filled with sports and pop singers, politics, war and greed, false religions and silly philosophies than it does about an Eternal Life filled with incredible wonders beyond the imaginings of mankind.

73

It is time for everyone on Earth to begin to take seriously the following statement: Humans must challenge their preconceptions or they will be destroyed by them. Where did your preconceptions come from? From other humans—not from God.

74
RECREATIONAL DRUGS AND ALCOHOL

These are poisonous substances that humans willingly put into their bodies hoping to experience a few moments of personal pleasure while knowing full well that they cause permanent physical damage to humans, and even death. Who among those of you who call yourselves enlightened, or spiritual, would partake willingly of these terrible things, knowing how dangerous they are and the fatal risk they pose?

75
CIGARETTES

When Sir Walter Raleigh introduced tobacco to the "civilized" world, nobody questioned it; nobody stood up and said:

> You want us to roll up a bundle of leaves, set one end on fire, place the other end in our mouths, and inhale deeply? You want us to put that poison into our bodies? That's insane!

76
TELEVISION

Most of what is offered on television as entertainment is abominable to God and should never be viewed by anyone who is truly serious about spiritual Awakening. Awakening will never happen if you continue to participate in television.

77

Contrary to popular New Age nonsense, God is not found within you, nor is God found in the rituals and dogmas of world religions and philosophies. God is not found in buildings where loud music is played and where shallow, well-practiced gestures of praise are displayed. Your Creator can only be found where TRUE DEVOTION is present, and your OWN Spiritual Awareness can be found within you without the aid of man-made religions.

78

ORGANIZED RELIGION

There has never been anything organized about it. The teachings of some of the spiritual leaders known throughout history may be useful in their own original forms, but to organize them into a religion is to automatically reduce them to a list of rules and regulations contrived by humans, thereby removing from them any semblance of their original Purity. As any TRUE seeker knows, when the purity of a spiritual concept is corrupted or diluted by the common philosophies of man, it is no longer Truth. In fact, it becomes dangerous, as evidenced by the role played by so-called organized religion in a great number of the wars waged throughout the history of this planet.

79

EARTH MUSIC

The words of most of the popular songs on Earth today perpetuate the practices and emotions of adolescent humans, with the result that the process of Spiritual Awakening in the human species is not just slowed, but reversed and set back by many centuries.

Some forms of music that have been conjured up over the past hundred years or so have vibratory qualities that are dangerous to both the Creation Frequency and to the human species—ask any physicist who is knowledgeable in energy vibration, frequency modulation and etc. It's not just the adolescent nature of the music itself—lyrics are thoughts and thoughts are energy—or the destructive frequencies being produced that are causing severe damage to the Creation Frequency, but the ACCEPTANCE of the music by most of the population of this planet.

The religious music found in most churches today is one of the major offenders due to its insipid portrayal of God, as well as its method of delivery to the audience. Do you really think that Heaven is going to be filled with boy bands and cute little girls in short skirts raising their hands and swaying to meaningless little songs—which, by the way, provide them with a tidy income—while immersing themselves in the culture of the world, and rationalizing their worldly way of life by claiming that it's all "for the lord?" Think again. Lies do not work with God.

Currently, there are no forms of music on planet Earth that are acceptable to God—NONE—and there are very few contemporary singer/songwriters on this entire world who are writing and singing God's Truth.

80

Angels ARE powerful Higher Beings that have been sent to Earth by the CREATOR to serve primarily as Messengers to the human species. They are not of this world. They are ALIEN to this world. They are from another world, and they are here for a purpose. That fact has not changed. It will not change. Angels seldom reveal themselves on Earth, and when they do it is often a terrifying sight and only for purposes of warning.

Angels DO walk among you—powerful Higher Beings. Their job is two fold: to destroy and to heal. To bring judgment upon errant human beings, and at the same time to heal and bring life to humans who are worthy, simply by the touch of their hand upon the one that needs healing.

There are many Guardian Angels, but there are only THREE Higher Being Angels on Earth at this time. The Higher Angels reveal themselves only when directed by God. Do not believe any humans who tell you they are Angels or healers; they will be lying. Those who claim to "channel" the Arch Angels, Michael, or Gabriel, or other Angels they have invented are lying, as well. Angels do NOT channel through human beings—that is a pathetically infantile claim. Angels do not NEED humans for ANYTHING, nor would Higher Being Angels ever condescend to the level of utilizing a human mind for communication. They are NOT here to communicate with humans. They are here to do GOD's work upon this little world.

But DO know that these Higher Ones watch all things. They act as directed. FEAR them. Be careful, as you may entertain one of these without being aware.

FEAR them. Far stranger things exist that have not yet been revealed.

Again, FEAR them. Be aware that Angels are not all "love and light" as some would have you believe. Angels will both correct and destroy. Be careful how you attempt to contact them—you do NOT play with Angels, even Guardian Angels. They are NOT your imaginary friends who sit on the edge of your bed for you to chitchat with—people who tell you that are not telling the truth.

Guardian Angels are wonderful creations and loving in their service to human beings, but they come and they go, doing only what they must. They are observers. They stay out of your life.

81

There is a Higher Source of Truth that will prevail in the end—one way or another. It is still possible for this world to survive, but those who really care must start the process by first changing themselves. Only then can they take their message to the world in order to change the world for the better. This must be done quickly.

82

There are five dark worlds remaining in the entire Cosmos. A date has been set for their annihilation, and that date is approaching rapidly. The only reason they have been allowed to remain active for as long as they have is that they are directly connected to a few Beings on planet Earth who are being allowed to carry to completion their roles in The Great Plan. When the work of these Beings is completed, all five dark worlds, including the inhabitants upon them, will be destroyed. No memory of who the inhabitants were or what they did will remain. Earth is one of the five. Unless the people of Earth dramatically and rapidly return to God, Earth will not survive, and all Earth humans will be annihilated.

83

The ONLY culture/race found on ALL other worlds everywhere in ALL universes, is the original HUMAN culture/race, which has retained the essence of the first Beings that were seeded on those worlds. Races do NOT exist on other worlds. The concepts of race and culture give rise to the adolescent religious agendas which, when combined with human emotions, are the principle sources of the negative energy frequencies that are responsible for destroying this planet. It is as simple as that. It has to do with ego. Humans must stop worshiping their skin color and their shallow emotions and return to TRUE Worship of God. Your race and your culture are irrelevant to God. Devotion to those two childish notions will only earn you pain in the next life.

84

Society has not progressed beyond its current primitive state largely because all vestiges of creativity and imagination have been choked out of the conscious minds of humans, and been replaced by the superficial nonsense that has consumed contemporary culture.

Even now, there are those who are reading this book through the distorted lens of religious bias and cultural nonsense. They are shaking their heads in disbelief at what they have read. Their ability to imagine anything more than what they have been taught by finite humans has become distorted by shallow nonsense, and TRUTH can no longer be discerned. IMAGINATION is not just about fantasy and make-believe. It is also the Spiritual Detector used to find the treasure under the trash—the TRUTH under the lies.

85

If you truly desire to develop the ability to create, i.e., turn water into wine, heal terrible diseases by simply asking them to go away, or even transport yourselves halfway across the galaxy to other worlds by merely thinking, then you must, AS AN ENTIRE CULTURE, make the decision to cease the childish nonsense you are so enamored of today, and begin to seek TRUTH in your communal whole. As long as there are those who continue to feed on the childish pabulum served up here, the adult main course will be withheld from you.

86

Religion and science can never be separated, despite the attempts by humanity to do just that. It can't be done. Effective science cannot be achieved without the inclusion of spiritual concepts, and religion can't be effective or explained without considering science. You can PROVE the concepts of religion with science if you open your mind to TRUTH instead of falling back on the silly, man-made, biased notions that have been taught over the years. A deeper understanding of science, and answers to questions that have baffled scientists for years will also be achieved by using the TRUTH found in God. When I say *religion* I do not mean the named denominations and churches; I mean the deeper metaphysical principles of religion, the spiritual nature of religion that has LITTLE to do with denominations or churches.

87

Where is Heaven—the main Heaven, that is? It is clearly ALIEN and not of this world. Heaven is a world much grander and more glorious than Earth, upon which reside Beings of such a supreme nature that they appear to be Angels of Heaven, and are therefore MISTAKEN for Angelic Beings.

88

How small-minded are those who refuse to believe there are no such things as Aliens, that Earth is the only planet in the entirety of the Cosmos that has people on it, that God does not exist, and that God does not watch over the Higher Dominion to make sure that The Great Plan is carried out to a T. How terribly primitive and closed-minded are they.

89

Human culture has been influenced by those of several other worlds over the past three million years. The worst of the problems you face today have little to do with how you have managed to bring them about, and everything to do with the rulers of the darkness who originated in the dark Systems long ago then came to this planet and diluted your SPIRIT with their own. Like oil and water, it did not mix very well. As a result of that action, many people on Earth today have the lineage of an evil nature. They are destined for failure, and some of them are in positions of authority on Earth, making them, in effect, a part of the rulers of darkness here on this world.

90

IF YOU UNDERSTAND NOTHING ELSE IN THIS BOOK, UNDERSTAND THIS:

The universe is not as complex and complicated as mankind has made it out to be. Humans seem to enjoy making problems out of things that were never meant to be problems in the first place. Let this knowledge break through to your INNER mind. Your conscious mind has buried your INNER mind under so many unnecessary layers that you can only see what the world has falsely presented to you for years. You MUST stop doing that if you are to survive. Allow your INNER mind to break through the layers. Look DEEP into the night sky TONIGHT and ponder the WONDERS that are truly there. Stare into the Cosmos and THINK about what might be staring back at you. Cease to be the Earth-bound creatures that you have allowed yourself to become, led on by the lies of those who would keep you in bondage forever. If you do not do this, Earth has no future.

91

As previously stated, human culture has not progressed beyond the primitive state it is in today largely because humans have choked any vestige of creativity and imagination out of their conscious minds, and replaced it with the superficial nonsense produced, extolled, and exemplified by the contemporary culture. Your children do not read the classics any more. They no longer live inside their minds and their imaginations have atrophied from lack of use. Your children worship soulless entertainers, empty pop singers, and immature sports figures as they kneel at the altar of the corrupt and unevolved culture. There is little hope for producing an enlightened culture out of the material present today. Shallow minds are crippling and destroying sacred Spirits.

92

When the frequency of an erroneous ego touches the frequency of Truth they will not bond, and the Promise that results from bonding with Truth will never be realized. That is why so many scientific theories devised by humans are incorrect. That is why so much time is being wasted on adolescent ideas that can go nowhere, instead of achieving great dreams by bonding with Truth.

93

Every THING in the universe is made of light and energy and frequency, and every thing is affected in some way when it comes into contact with some other thing. Since the frequency of each thing is unique, and causes that thing to either bond with or repel whatever it touches, would not a person—who is also a thing—by accepting TRUTH, also bond to TRUTH, resonate with TRUTH, and attain the promise of that TRUTH?

On the other hand, if a person rejects TRUTH—refuses to bond and resonate with TRUTH—is it not logical that the promise that comes with the acceptance of TRUTH would be unattainable for the person who rejected it? Every thing has a frequency. TRUTH is a frequency. If the frequency of your personal decision rejects the TRUTH, there can be no bonding of the energy to produce the Promise. In effect, you will repel TRUTH away from you. If the frequency of your decision is one of acceptance of TRUTH, you will attract TRUTH to you, and then the frequency of TRUTH will bond comfortably with that frequency of decision, thereby producing the NEW frequency of the Promise.

94

Nearly everything that is done in the fields of science, medicine, and technology today would have been labeled witchcraft not too long ago; even something as simple as a cheap ballpoint pen. If you had been caught with such a pen in your possession five hundred years ago, you might have been burnt at the stake for having a magical device. As late as the 1800s, the words science and sorcery were nearly synonymous. At one time, science and religion worked hand in hand to understand the world and the cosmos. Today, they are often at odds with each other as misguided, dishonest, and immature human beings from both camps, science and religion, rely on false information to perpetuate the same nonsense. In fact, all of the fear and mistrust on both sides is totally unfounded by fact. The hatred and jealousy found today among the immature minds of both the scientists and the religious are baseless and unsupported by any evidence whatsoever. Both sides are being childish at the cost of human advancement on Planet Earth and the destruction of the Jewel of U48.

95

You put so much trust and faith in your simple science, but your science cannot tread the path that will soon be created for this world. Your science does not have the information or the technology to survive what is to come. You MUST return to God and learn to use a higher form of reasoning, Spiritual Science, by which all things find their being. If you do so without delay, God may open vast resources of knowledge beyond your imagination. You must make the first step.

96

Sometimes the best way to live at peace with others is to simply no longer associate with them. Why do you think the saints liked living with the birds and animals of Nature rather than with other people? Earth people are not the easiest creatures to get along with. Science, religion, and wisdom cannot function properly if the atmosphere in which they are deployed is a hostile one. That is why there is still a division between the would-be practitioners of those three disciplines today. Not one of them has the courage to alter their erroneous assumptions and get along with the others.

97

When a human walks the path of Nature, resonating the peaceful energies of the path, and returning to the same energy frequencies he once held in purity, he will eventually become indistinguishable from all of Nature around him. Once he hooks into the supernatural, it no longer frightens him, and he no longer frightens Nature. He blends and becomes a veritable part of Nature.

98

NATURE is the single most important and sacred Icon designed by and for God. To respect Nature is to gain the assurance of receiving a great reward in the afterlife. By respect for Nature, it is not meant that you are to join any of the popular contemporary environmentalist groups; their main reasons for existence are ego and financial gain—avoid all groups. Respect for Nature is when YOU spend time alone with Mother Nature in the privacy of your own garden, the forest, in the desert, by the sea, or wherever you can feel close to Her. It is when the electrons of your body spin out around you for thousands of feet, communing with the electrons of the Creation of God: Sentient, Living, Nature.

If you insist upon meditating, you need to be quiet. Never use a mantra; you can't hear the voice of God or of Mother Nature if you're droning on in some language you don't understand. You need to just be quiet and listen. Listen. Listen. God will contact you if you listen, but you have to REALLY listen. You spend so much time in your culture being noisy and not listening. Humans are noisy, even in so-called meditation. That just doesn't make sense.

99

Although God is the Creator of all, He allows Earth to be under the control of Mother Nature, who controls all Nature everywhere, and much more. Here on Earth, it's all about Mother Nature. Listen for her. Listen to her. She will speak to your conscious mind and you can sense in your gut what she is saying. Take her advice when she gives it. Do what she tells you to do. Forget all the silly stuff that you might have been told you must do in order to become a person in tune with Nature—a Nature person. Just be quiet and listen to the voice of Nature, because Mother is that voice.

100

Nature IS wonder-filled, with or without your presence in it. Nothing you can do will faze Mother Nature in any way, so stop trying to invoke this and affirm that. Quit doing those absurd witchcraft spells that accomplish nothing. Someone told you that they are good for this or that, and you've gone along with it because you think people will notice you and think you are special. A REAL Nature person doesn't need spells and costumes and tarot cards or any of the latest faddish props. A REAL Nature person needs only Nature. If you are in sync with Mother Nature; if you are LISTENING to her and not droning out some human-devised mantra; if you LOVE her and respect who she is and what she does and you NEVER try to control her, or think that you can—because Nature belongs to HER and not to you—then she will work with you in ways you have never imagined. Mother Nature will turn her back on you if you attempt to control her.

101

Mother Nature is NOT what many have been trying to convince the public she is, regardless of how she has been portrayed, regardless of whatever "goddess" she has been said to be. Mother Nature is a wonderful and precious Being. She is both a Lover and a Destroyer, but her true ESSENCE is one of compassion for all creation, even humans, but those humans must agree with her and follow her rules and not make up their own. Compassion comes only as the result of obedience. A world that refuses to obey the Laws of God will be removed. That has always been the case. It always will be.

102

Bees and ants and dragonflies are all more than just common sights in a garden. They are living, sentient Beings of great WORTH to this tiny world. I can see them—their auras explode and mingle with everything around them. If there's one thing I want the readers of this book to get, it's the FACT that NOTHING is as it appears to be on the outside—nothing in this physical life. Nothing. Do you wish to SEE Faeries? To speak with Nature Beings? Then you must stop living as society has designed you to live, and let your SPIRIT come to the surface of your physical shell. You cannot dwell in a world of criminals, loud music, profane activity, common culture, and lies and still expect to walk with Angels or Faeries or Saints. It is impossible.

103

Your salvation comes not in the rituals and costumes of an invented religion, but in the middle of a hot, arid desert when you open your eyes for the very first time and SEE the infinity of LIFE around you.

104

There are eight locations found here on Earth that are most beloved by God and by Mother Nature. Each one of these sacred locations has been given a Stone of Great Power. These stones, called Home Stones, are complex energy transformers, dynamos of great power, that gather and focus specific, concentrated frequencies of energy directly from the massive stream of the Creation Frequency that blanket the entire Earth, and seep down to the very core of this planet to deliver a constant flow of essential information from the Cosmos. Were these stones to be removed, all life on Earth would perish within moments.

The Home Stones are found in Annica Gardens, Missouri, USA; Laggan, Scotland; Habo, Sweden; Great Torrington, England; Bethlehem, Israel; Derry, Ireland; Beaminster Wessex/Dorset, England; and Dwarka, India.

The exact locations of the stones cannot be revealed here, but if you were to visit the regions where the stones lie, you would feel the PRESENCE of the energy that saturates the areas surrounding them. Three of the stones, including the Annica Gardens stone, are situated in highly secured locations that are off limits to the general public and well-guarded, but the other stones rest totally in the open and can be walked by without even knowing it.

105
GBTG

Cultural identities represented by initials seem to be so important on this tiny planet, but if you wish to represent TRUTH, you should disregard meaningless labels that often so often represent societal perversions and reinforce artificial barriers and definitions. Instead, adopt the label of TRUTH, THE initials that represent the TRUE GOD. If you wish to declare an identity, be part of a movement, belong to a community, then let it be the GBTG Movement, the GBTG Community. Human society is destroying itself. If you do not leave behind the shallow teachings of the culture and Get Back To God, you will be no more. You are not meant to get back to religion, but to Get Back To God. Only God.

Entries 106–111
PRACTICLE APPLICATION

106
THE SPIRITUAL STEPS OF PURE WORSHIP: WHERE ARE YOU?

STEP 1

Imagine a stairway going upward into the sky, and each step represents a level of personal growth and Awakening. At the very bottom of this stairway, the lowest step is labeled the *Baser World* or *Humanity.* This is the generic, mundane mass of humanity in its average state of being—the common man or woman on the street in any city in any country. Regardless of race, gender, physical condition or culture, everyone starts off on this level. Many stay on this level for the full length of their lives, never progressing upward in understanding, or development toward the culmination of the Awakened Spiritual Being they were created to become.

As the lowest level on the stairs, this one represents what one might call the dull ones—the ones who have no desire or ambition to achieve a heightened state of being; those who are content with the inane fodder of the culture in which they reside; those who follow the fads and fashions of the world, watch the latest movies, become fanatic sports fans, belong to political parties with a passion, and/or consider their race and culture to be of more importance than their faith in God.

These unevolved, superficial minds are the clones of the culture whose existence relies on the physical and not the spiritual. Pop music and movie stars, fads and fashions, makeup and clothes, basketball players and TV shows, alcohol and drugs—these are some of the things that mean the most to these people who are content to remain in a state of shallow, non-evolution within the Baser World.

It is a sad fact that the vast majority of humans on this world at this time fall into this category.

STEP 2

A Choice Is Made To Reject Human Cultural Beliefs, Rituals, Philosophies. The meaning of this is simple; you wake up one day realizing that just about everything you have done during your life is worthless, that most of what you have been taught is untrue, and that a large percentage of what you have believed to be important, isn't. You KNOW that NONE of the material of the baser world-nature is REALLY important, and most of the time you have spent in it and with it has been a gigantic waste of effort, emotion, belief, health, energy and money. You begin to REALIZE that there is something MORE to life than all of the embarrassing, adolescent nonsense you have been immersing yourself in for years, simply because that nonsense is popular with the culture in which you live. Therefore, you make the conscious decision to REJECT EVERYTHING society has to offer, and empty your mind of everything that was ever taught to you.

Now you find yourself dramatically OPENED to TRUTHS that you never knew before—that you never even considered before—because you were always listening to other people who were feeding you their opinions and agendas and you were NOT hearing anything else. But how do you know what those REAL TRUTHS are?

STEP 3

Daily Prayer—Speaking To God For Guidance. You begin to PRAY on a daily basis.

Most people who are on the first step of growth seldom if ever pray, and when they do it is for superficial reasons that gratify ego or reward them in a physical way. Some on the second step might offer prayers that were taught to them in church, usually just reciting them from memory with no thought for how they may or may not be relevant in their own life. But on this third step of the stairway your prayer has developed a deeper nature. You are beginning to hold full conversations with God. You talk to God as you would talk to your father or your mother or your brother or sister—as if God is your best friend.

What do you talk about? You talk about what you need to do to go HIGHER on the stairs. Not because it is demanded of you but because you WANT to do it. You ask God for GUIDANCE in your life that will move you forward and upward, not backward and downward to where you have been wallowing for years—down to where there is absolutely NOTHING for you.

STEP 4

After you have talked to God for a little while, and asked your questions, you will find yourself on the fourth step: *Listening in Silence To Receive Answers.* This is where your Awakening really begins. After you have adopted a life of regular, personal prayer, then you need to become SILENT and LISTEN for God's answer. God will deliver the guidance you seek to your mind, but you need to become silent so you can hear it. If you have human music or videos or computer articles—or any distractions—running around in your brain you will never hear the guidance; you will never receive the answers. Awakening BEGINS the very moment those first few words of guidance come breaking through. Notice the capital letters; you are not in an Awakened state just because you pray and receive Guidance from God. Your Awakening has only begun.

STEP 5

Recognition of the Mysteries — Open To Hearing God's Spirit Daily. Many things are going on at this level. Your mind is now open to possibilities you never considered before, and you begin to realize that just because people have told you something about God and the Ways of God, you come to see that just because a religion teaches this, that, or the other, there always remains the possibility that ALL of what you have been taught is incorrect, or at least LACKING in TRUTH and PURITY. After all, even the Bible says that God is a MYSTERY and that no one can ever know God's thoughts or His plans for the future. No human knows how it will all end up in the Last Days. So why is it that the religions all believe that they have the final word on what God is thinking and planning for this little world? That just doesn't make sense. How can any one group know that their way is the only way? NO HUMAN KNOWS FOR SURE.

At this level of your ascent, you are Awakening to the HONEST realization that you don't have a clue, so you need to continue to talk to God and LISTEN to what God says back to you—in your mind of course, inside your conscience. You will never hear God speaking audibly to you; no human has in thousands of years, and those who say they have are lying.

Other questions will begin to pop into your head such as:

- If God's Thoughts and Ways are all a mystery, how can I TRULY understand any of this beyond a base level of understanding?
- How can I ask God the right questions if everything is a Mystery?
- How can I KNOW that the answers I receive are REAL or just imagined?

STEP 6

With that, you will find yourself rising to the sixth step: *Total Faith and Undeniable Belief.*

Your Awakening has blossomed dramatically and you have acquired the desire and the ability to do nothing without guidance from God. You are able to say to God:

> It doesn't matter. I'm done asking questions and worrying about all of this. I am just going to keep my mouth shut and my mind open to whatever You direct me to do, and I am going to just DO IT without question. I'm throwing out everything I've ever been told—because I KNOW it isn't accurate. I SEE that now, and I am going to just go forward from this point. This is the point of no return. This is the point of BLIND FAITH—COMPLETE FAITH IN GOD ALONE, WHO IS GREATER THAN ALL EARTH RELIGIONS THAT HAVE BEEN DEVISED THROUGHOUT THE CENTURIES.

STEP 7

The seventh and highest step on the stairway that a human being can achieve: *Deep Silence.*

Above this step are the realms of the Angels, and even of God Himself—realms you can never enter. On this step you SHOULD achieve a higher level of Awakening, that is, of course, unless you get crazy and retreat back toward the first step and the Baser World. When you reach this seventh step of DEEP SILENCE you will IMMERSE YOURSELF TOTALLY IN FAITH AND IN AWARENESS OF THE CLOSENESS OF GOD WHO IS ALWAYS NEAR YOU—RIGHT NEXT TO YOU—EVERY MOMENT OF EVERY DAY YOU ARE HERE.

This step is called the level of DEEP SILENCE because you no longer feel the need for any of the noise or entertainments of this world, and you have reached the point in your growth that you no longer need to ask the questions you used to ask of God. This is not the same as so-called meditation; you have gone far beyond such simplistic Earth disciplines which often bring more confusion and frustration than help. You can now simply bask in the DEEP SILENCE of your FAITH that produces the REAL awareness of God's constant Presence.

This seventh step is the GOAL for all to achieve. Remember, scriptures from nearly every religion on Earth tell us that God is a Spirit and you must worship Him in Spirit and in Truth. It is in this state of DEEP SILENCE that you are able to allow your own Spirit to sense the Spirit that is God. But you MUST be sure that you have left the other six steps behind you, for if you dwell on any one of them, this seventh step will not be possible.

Each step takes you further from this world and its culture, and you MUST remove the culture of the world completely from your life in order to commune with God, for God cannot be present where any part of this profane culture resides. This is PURE TRUTH. It is a matter of Spiritual Physics. The Frequency that is the Spirit of God does not blend with the frequency that is the common culture. The two are like oil and water. Your Spirit communing with God is like a clear, fresh, mountain stream merging with another into one. When you are capable of realizing that state of Being, you will have no use for any further advice from any person, church, religion, philosophy or opinion on this world. You will be content to sit outdoors in your garden, to commune with the mystical Beings who reside there, to stare up into the sky, to feel the

Presence of the Spirit of the Creator who is your true God—content to be at one with the holy SILENCE of eternity.

STEPS EIGHT AND NINE

There are two more steps on the Worship Stairway: eight, Angels; and nine, GOD. These are the MYSTERY REALMS OF THE HIGHER BEINGS where no human can ever go; regions that no human can define or even discuss, for no human has ever seen or experienced them. The human steps stop at the seventh step of DEEP SILENCE, where monks and nuns reside and where the Awakened Ones of this world exist, sharing the experience of their own Awakening with those who have not yet gained the seventh step. How do you know that you have reached the seventh step? You will know it and you will never tell anyone that you have achieved it, as that would be an act of pure ego that would push you back down the stairway, perhaps all the way to the bottom.

These Spiritual Steps of Pure Worship comprise all the teachings required to guide human spiritual growth, and are everything that any religion needs to be. No costumes, no music, no meeting places or rituals—just the bare bones of a devotional practice that humanity was given at their Genesis and that they have warped and misused ever since.

107
How Shall You Live?

Do you know WHO you are or where you came from? Many humans seem to gravitate toward Nature and things of Nature, motivated by the desire to resonate with the frequencies emitted by Nature that was encoded within the original DNA of human beings.

One of the universal laws is the Law of Rhythm, which states that the bodies of all things, including humans, have a unique and inherent natural rhythm that directs who they are and how they relate to all things around them, especially Nature. This is not the same as the so-called Biorhythm fad you probably heard about back in the 1970s; this is the true biorhythmic nature of a human being. Unlike the old fad, there is no chart or calculator one can mass-produce for everyone to study. True biorhythmic frequencies are random and individualized to each person and to their situation at any given moment of any day. They are FELT, and can never be charted.

If a person's biorhythms are in full swing, that person is healthy, happy, emotionally stable, and pretty much guaranteed a long life. Even the concept of prosperity enters into this picture because when a person is operating at his or her physiological best, then that person's mind is also functioning at top levels, insuring that most of that person's decisions and experiences will be positive, leading to success in just about everything, including wealth and prosperity. It just makes sense.

On the other hand, if a person's biorhythms are at a low point, then his or her health, happiness, emotions, and wellbeing will be negatively affected. Bottom line—biorhythms are a big part of who a human is.

They explain much about you, and they can be effected by outside influences. Biorhythmic resonance improves in outdoor settings of wild Nature.

During the Creation of the planet itself, long before humans were placed here, God Seeded the attributes and energy frequencies of specific designs into the life Spirit of the sentient Earth Body. It is those frequencies that govern all Life and Nature on Earth forever, energized by the greater power of the Creation Frequency. Because of those attributes and frequencies, Nature affects every human on every level. Consider how a person's emotions, even a person's blood pressure is affected by the full Moon. Changing barometric pressure and wind does the same thing and can bring on headaches; over exposure to the rays of the sun causes terrible sunburn. The list goes on.

The reason Nature affects humans is because humans are basically Nature beings, and when a humans energy frequencies are properly attuned to Nature, that human can resonate with the frequencies of Nature. When a human is removed from Nature, his frequencies become distorted and join with whatever unnatural frequencies surround him. When human beings were Seeded on Earth and given life, they were created to BE a Nature people. They were created to react to and interact with the energy frequencies emitted by Nature. Those frequencies were built into every human as an integral part. Why? Because in order for humans to reach their highest potential they need to resonate at a frequency similar to the Primary Frequency found in Nature.

In the beginning this was not a problem, but as time passed and mankind got further away from the

Universal Principles of God and Nature, the frequencies of mankind became diluted and changed dramatically into what is found today. In their current state, those frequencies are not strong enough to bring about the oneness with Nature that is necessary for mankind to progress to a Higher State. In fact, as the frequencies continue to be diluted by the distortions found within human culture, mankind is in imminent danger of falling into a state of anarchy, delusion, and primitive self-destruction—it is only a matter of very little time. Unless something dramatic happens soon to block the flow of corruption that humans are allowing into their physical and spiritual makeup, humans will destroy themselves.

Somewhere on the Internet there is a store where you can purchase a long chart—eight feet by three feet—depicting the entirety of human history for the past few thousand years. It doesn't include the true beginnings of humans on this world of course, only the guesswork of human scientists. Human history is represented on this chart by a long, straight line, with so-called Cave Men at one end, and Today at the opposite end. Various important events in history are placed along the line—the discovery of fire, ancient Egypt, the Golden Age of Greece, the Roman Empire, the Dark Ages, the Renaissance, etc., all down the line until you get to the modern era with the Ages of Industry and Technology where humans are today.

Because of the level of the technology in use today, Humanity thinks it is quite advanced, but on that eight-foot line of human history, the Ages of Industry and Technology take up only TWO INCHES. On the chart, humanity is illustrated by EIGHT FEET of wallowing in the mud, sleeping in grass huts, running from predators, and defecating in the woods. Only two inches represent all of the technological advancement humans have today, including indoor plumbing. At the rate human society is going right now, less than one-sixteenth of one inch will be added to the eight-foot chart before humanity ceases to exist on this world. What does that say about mankind?

Humans are born into Nature and humans will die in Nature. All of Nature's laws apply to humans, and yet they fight against Nature with nearly everything they do. As I stated earlier, God and Nature are inseparable. Man was meant to be joined with Nature and, therefore, to God, forever. That is not working out. Incidentally, the last two inches on that chart, the Ages of Industry and Technology, are nothing to brag about. Those accomplishments should have been achieved by Earth humans thousands of years ago, but humans were too busy playing politics, deifying their races and body colors, fighting wars, and supporting celebrities to advance along with the rest of the universe.

Again, this world is destined to destroy itself in a very short time unless the heart of the culture changes dramatically, and changes soon. Human beings are no longer following the laws of Nature that were placed inside them at their Creation. Because of that they are no longer resonating with the correct energy frequencies that come with following those Laws. In fact, almost everything produced by humans within the contemporary culture represents pretty much the direct opposite of the Laws. In effect, humans are very rapidly destroying themselves ON PURPOSE, and they are lying to themselves about the worth of it all. What kind of logic is that?

Humanity is so impressed by it's low-grade technological achievements. They are so comfortable in their air-conditioned homes, and so pleased with their little cars that take them everywhere they go. Their movies and entertainments drip with the sweet honey of the violence and bloodshed they so enjoy. They lay their worship at the feet of the false, profane gods they call sports heroes, pop musicians, movie stars, and corrupt politicians driven by radical agendas. Their music is of a primal beat, with primitive messages of human weaknesses strewn liberally throughout the lyrics, and the musicians are gaudy automatons of false emotions and superficial desires. They are spoiled by the incredible assortment of fashions and clothing, including garments that allow them to go outside in all kinds of weather, and to do it with style in the latest expensive and inane fashions. Oh, they are really something.

It wasn't so long ago that your ancestors huddled around fires that often took them hours to build while shivering inside damp, cold caves, just to stay safe from predators—both animal and, of course, human.

Your homes are now filled with push-button gadgetry—televisions, toasters, home entertainment centers, washing machines, computers, indoor plumbing, electric lights and heating, smart phones. These things are all so common to you that you don't even think about them any more, except when they break down or stop working, and then you have to interrupt your routine and call in a repairman to fix them, or you simply throw them away and replace them with the newest models. What a terrible inconvenience to your day.

Where would you be without your cars and trucks, motorcycles, and RVs; what about the airplanes that fly you halfway across the country in a couple of hours? It took your not-so-distant ancestors weeks and sometimes months traveling in wagons and on foot just to go a few miles, taunted, harassed, and threatened the whole way by ferocious animals and other evil human beings, trying to kill them just for the few material possessions they carried.

Yes, you are a technology-dependent people today. But you are not a people connected just to your antique gadgets and gizmos; you are also, deep inside, still connected to Nature. That is the way God designed you to be. It is still inside there somewhere; you just don't think about it much. You have buried it so deep inside you that you can't feel it any more.

Humans were not born with computers plugged into their orifices. In fact, computers and technology are really only a very small part of what you have become, not who you are. If you take away all of the computers, airplanes, smart phones, washing machines—all of the inventions and man-made conveniences—you are wild Nature Beings again. In other words, you are just two inches away from being uncivilized pagans! But if you were to loose your gadgets now, you would not be able to survive a week in the wilds of Nature because your own Nature frequencies lie dormant.

And as much as their advanced technology leads some people to believe that they have come so far as a species, they really haven't. They've only covered over it, put on a disguise of shiny metal and plastic. Life on the outside is nothing more than an illusion manufactured to please and appease the human ego. In fact, they have not been advancing at all; they have been wallowing in the same stagnant pond of mediocrity for centuries. HEAR ME: something must be done soon to change that.

108

LIVE AS NATURE LIVES

How many of you are aware that Nature itself is controlled by rhythms? I call these rhythms the Tides of Nature, for their resemblance to the ebbing and flowing tides of the ocean. There are four of these Rhythms, and they are associated with the Seasons of the Earth year, and even though they are the Rhythms of Nature, they have a strong influence on both the conscious and the subconscious lives of human beings.

If you learn to flow with these four Seasonal Tides as you were always meant to, you will benefit greatly, and you will be more able to halt the deterioration of the Creation Frequency—which is occurring rapidly even as I write this—and to aid in its healing. The section that follows is intended to instruct you in the replication of these Tides within your own life.

THE GROWING TIDE: MARCH THROUGH JUNE

The Growing Tide is the tide of springtime, when all of the trees begin to leaf out and the lawns start to green up. Some of you will till up the Earth for your gardens during this Tide. It is the particular time of year that has been designed to be a time of intense life and energy, a time when things are supposed to grow. If you drop a seed on the ground during the Growing Tide, there is almost nothing you can do to stop it from growing. You can't expect the same success during December; that's because December isn't part of the Growing Tide—it's part of a different Tide.

The Rhythm of Nature assures successful and rapid growth during this particular cycle, as it has for millions of years with or without mankind's interference, and it will continue to do so. Call it science, physics, Growing Tide, or whatever, the bottom line is that it is a law of science and it has to happen. Mother Nature controls it and nothing on this world can stop it, for it is the specific Tide that regulates growth for this world.

The Growing Tide touches every living thing on Earth. It is a powerful energy force that was set into motion at the beginning of time, and continues to influence all that you are as a species. The early Egyptian civilizations referred to this powerful energy FORCE as *Heka*, a word that came to mean a form of powerful magic or energy force that controls all life.

There was a TV program back in the 1970s called Connections. The premise of the show was that each bit of technology in use today came about as a result of one tiny little something having been invented or introduced sometime in the past centuries, such as a small brass rivet that was first introduced in 1145 AD, going through twenty different alterations and adaptations, and finally morphing into the left headlight on the Mars Rover. That same process gave rise to the names of the ancient gods and goddesses of Earth. It's a form of what has become known as the Butterfly Effect, that is, the principle that expresses the idea that you can't really do ANYTHING without your anything BECOMING something entirely different in the future. Think about that before you DO anything, because anything you DO will have consequences. It will ultimately PRODUCE results that are beyond your imagination.

That is the purpose of all four of the Tides under Mother Nature's control. Everything in Nature produces something that in turn produces something else, and ALL of it in some way, sooner or later, affects human beings. Conversely human beings produce things that affect Nature.

Here is something to think about: If this Growing Tide affects every physical aspect of every living thing—which it does—then is it possible that it might also affect things of a non-physical nature, like your thoughts, emotions, desires, dreams, and even your intuitive abilities and your spiritual decisions? That's a very good question.

The Growing Tide is a Tide of expansion. Just as the tiny seed you plant in the spring grows and expands into a giant Oak tree, your dreams and desires can also be planted during this time of the year, and you can watch those dreams and desires grow and expand as well.

The season of the Growing Tide is the best time of year to start new projects you may have been thinking about for perhaps many years. It is the best time to move into a new house—which is analogous to planting the seed of your family into new soil. It is the best time of the year to change careers.

It isn't an accident that spring-cleaning rituals happen in spring, because that is when the Rhythm of Nature's Growing Tide comes to the surface and gently nudges you to do that sort of thing. This has been going on for thousands of years. If you didn't have a house, you would be cleaning your cave.

It is also the best time of the year to begin new relationships. That's why there are so many June weddings. Strong relationships get started, get fed, and begin to grow during this Season.

It is the best time to dream big dreams and to set goals for the future, to really sit down and decide who you are and where you want to be ten or twenty years from now, and make the plans for achieving your goals. Everything you dream, or every goal you set, is like a little seed you plant that can't help but grow during this time of year—if you water it; this is a Universal Law that cannot fail regardless of what you do, or what comes against you. It MUST work. It has no choice in the matter.

THE HARVEST TIDE: MIDSUMMER SOLSTICE THROUGH SEPTEMBER

When you think of the word harvest, most of you will probably think of September, or the beginning of autumn. You might think of cutting hay, gathering fruit or nuts, or tilling up your own family garden. That is what humans on this planet have come to recognize as harvest time.

The Harvest *Tide*, however, is different from harvest *time*. This natural Tide is the energy and life FORCE that empowers the final harvest during harvest time. It is the force that brings the harvest to fruition. The TRUE harvest in Nature isn't just a September thing; it is an on-going process that gives and gives all summer long. You start picking some fruits and vegetables in early summer, and you continue until summer has ended.

The word fruition comes from the root word, fruit. So bringing something to fruition means to ripen something to its final state of perfection, when it can then be pulled from the vine—harvested—so it can be eaten or put to use. IT HAS MATURED INTO WHAT IT WAS MEANT TO BECOME. The Harvest Tide is the Tide that brings all things to fulfillment.

As with all of these natural Tides, this particular Tide of Harvest affects more than just crops. It affects deeper metaphysical principles and levels of existence.

The time from the summer solstice to the fall equinox—about 21 June, to about 22 September, but the exact date varies from year to year—is the time when the seeds of your dreams, goals, relationships and projects that you planted during the Growing Tide, begin to bear fruit. There is something about the energy of this Tide that makes it all happen, and this is where the pay-off begins. If you started a project last January, then this time of year holds your best chance for the completion of that project. If you began a new friendship, you will find that your friendship will not only grow to new heights during this time of year, but that your new friend may now be proving to be the best friend you have ever had. The friendship will ripen and the fruit will be sweet. If you have been struggling with learning something new, you will suddenly get it.

This is the time of the year when things happen. When dreams come true. When rewards are reaped. When everything makes sense. However, you will have had to plant the seed of your dream during the Growing Tide, because that is the way the natural forces of this planet work. Everything in this universe has a rhythm to it. The early people knew this and planned accordingly. If you learn to plan your activities, business prospects, real estate deals, everything, around these natural Tides, you will witness amazing results.

THE LOW TIDE: THE END OF SEPTEMBER TO THE END OF DECEMBER

The Low Tide is when all of Nature takes a nap. Trees, grass, wild animals, and gardens all start to slow down. The crops are in, and the ripened fruits are picked and stored away. So, too, does the life force of a human being enter into a quieter, more reflective state at this time of the year.

As the weather cools, humans move indoors to begin their time of hibernation, not unlike the bears who have begun theirs. Unlike the bears, who will spend this time in sleep, the mental energies of humans are at a state of high alert even as their bodies begin to slow down physically. The human mind and thought processes are actually more alert and active during this Tide than at other times.

This is the time of year during which you might want to look inward to your spiritual life. This is the time to take stock of where you are on your spiritual journey—to reflect where you have been, where you are, and where you want to be. If you have made little or no progress, then this is a good time for personal study and research. Branch out a little and broaden your knowledge of art, history, astronomy, and the deeper things of life on Earth. Read new books, ones that are worthy of your time and energy and will add strength to your true being.

Like the animals, humans too, should be slowing down at this time of year. It's cold outside, and you should be inside reading books and spending more time in prayer and reflection. One of the problems modern humans have, though, is that their overly busy society has made that almost impossible. They cannot just go into hibernation, because the job goes on. The organizations they belong to still hold meetings. Their children's schools still have activities. These things all fight against the natural order of things, so it is difficult to truly observe the Low Tide Rhythm of Nature. You must, however, try to do so as much as possible. The Divine Order of Nature directs the body to slow down during this season.

If your job is mostly mental or otherwise physically undemanding, that's fine, because that's within the dictates of the Low Tide Season. This is the time of year to store away a reserve of physical energy, so for the sake of your health, slow your body down a bit if you can. It is the natural thing to do.

Your body and your inner Being hasn't forgotten, or somehow turned off these ancient Tides just because the industrialized culture has moved away from the Natural Rhythm of life. That will never happen. These Laws come directly from God and cannot be altered, amended, or changed in any way.

THE TIDE OF THE WIND OR THE FLOWING TIDE: CHRISTMAS TO THE SPRING EQUINOX

I do not call this the Tide of The Wind because it is the windy season of the year—although it can be. It is called the Tide of the Wind because wind is a powerful force for erosion, and as the constant winds scour the surface of the Earth, this season is of cleansing.

The wind erodes the rocks and cliffs. It shifts the desert sands, removing all footprints and other signs of life from the surface of the dunes. The flowing tide of the ocean buries or reveals rocks and shells and even giant boulders, or breaks them into pieces, or picks them up and deposits them elsewhere.

Just as the flowing sea or the blowing wind can remove or sweep away all evidence of the past, so can you; and this is the time of year to do it. You have no doubt heard the phrase, *to turn over a new leaf*; that is just what each human being needs to do. To turn over a new leaf means to CHANGE the way things are and to make something new and beneficial for your life. To change often means to return to a practice that once WORKED for you, but that you removed from your life because of many years of cultural pressure, politically correct nonsense, or the outright lies from a false-faced society. It means throwing out the garbage of worthless attitudes, opinions, and phony images you have collected from friends, teachers, and even a few spiritual leaders of dubious character. It means that it is time for you to re-discover who you REALLY are on the inside and to break the mold this world has forced you into.

Contrary to a corny song that was popular in the 70s, you are NOT the world. This world is a bad dream being played out in the minds of billions of people all over this globe. Just because the majority of people are living this nightmare, does not make the nightmare REAL, nor does it make it DESIRABLE for you to imitate. There are a select few among the mass of humanity who will come to this realization and who will blossom into the Beings that they were meant to be, and it is a core intent of this book to Awaken within those few Spirits the driving desire to do just that.

The Season of the Tide of the Wind is the time for you to prepare the beds of your mental and spiritual garden for planting in the Season of the Growing Tide.

In order to prepare a garden bed for planting, the old soil must be cleansed and renewed, the weeds must be removed, rocks and sticks need to be tossed away. The dirt must be tilled, the beds prepared, and plans made and plotted out of how and where you are going to plant every type of seed in the renewed garden space. These acts are all within full agreement of the Flowing Tide, the Tide Of The Wind.

As humans, you can take advantage of the energy found within this Tide, for Nature releases its ENERGY in huge amounts during this Season. So it really is a good time to clean your house, to prepare your garden beds, to go through your garage or boxes or drawers, to organize your cupboards, to take used clothing to the Goodwill store. It is a statistical fact that organizations like Goodwill and Salvation Army take in twice as much surplus at this time of year as they do at any other time. Is that a coincidence? I think not.

This Tide also has a strong influence on human relationships; More precisely, on leaving a relationship. The natural energies are aligned in such a way as to make this the time of the year to do so. The subject of human relationships is one of the most popular and complex to ponder on Planet Earth. To be honest, the whole thing is rather silly and a bit ponderous at times. Quite frankly, most people on this world do not know how to have a TRUE relationship, as TRUE relationships do not begin here; they can only begin in the Spirit Form. That is why so many of you have such a hard time in this area, and why so many relationships on Earth are often unpleasant. You fall in love with another Earth human who is in no way related to you in terms of Spirit or eternity. When the newness wears off and the object of your affection is revealed as the TRUE person they really are, it is not always a pleasant discovery. After a few years of marriage on Earth, many humans begin to regret marrying the person they did, and long to find the so-called soul mate that they feel is still out there somewhere. And that feeling is not incorrect. Others chose to flow with the Tides of Nature and all worked out well for them.

The reality is that there are some marriages that are eternal relationships between two Spirit Beings, but most on Earth are not. Most marriages on Earth are not spiritually permanent, and that includes even the few that seem to be exemplary when compared to the others in this world. God has created the perfect person for you to marry—IF you are to marry—and that person WILL come into your life at exactly the time they are supposed to in order for you to find one another. However, most humans do not wait for that to happen. They get impatient and they fall for the first good-looking guy with muscles and hard abs that comes along. They fall for the first girl who is cute and willing to have sex with them on the first date. They fall for someone their cultural/social/racial circle has arranged for them to marry. Church groups are terribly guilty of this. Many people marry simply because they feel pressured by their friends in their Church.

The bottom line is that every human has many TRUE friends and relatives back Home from whence they came. You who are reading this book have a soul mate or an eternal soul friend who is waiting for you either back Home, or here on this world inside a physical body. If you have blown a physical opportunity already, take heart, situations can change, if not on this world, then when you return Home.

If you are going to break off a bad relationship,

this is the best time of the year to do so. If you are in an abusive one, you need to break it off. It could be that your true Anam Cara, as the Celts call them, has already found you and is waiting patiently for you to change your bad situation so they can make themselves known to you. Hopefully you will recognize that when it finally happens

Consider all the factors of your life and the practicalities of changing the way things are into something dramatically different just because of a romantic feeling. Sometimes it is destined by God that you just stay the way you are until you get back Home, because there are situations down here that must not be tampered with; to do so would disrupt The Great Plan in some way, and change is just not practical. You need to let God make the final decisions for you in those cases, and those cases should be evident by the simple application of logic and common sense.

Regarding things that are not romantic in nature, if you are going to quit your job, sell off stocks, change a real estate agent; if you are wanting to stop anything, break a habit, that sort of thing, this is the time of year to do it. This is the CLEANSING time. It is the time of REMOVAL—those are the key words you should be using during this Tide.

This is also the Tide during which a person should do a little of that SPIRITUAL housecleaning that was mentioned earlier. I don't want you to forget about that. It is the perfect time to dump prejudices, opinions, attitudes, and shallow convictions you know to be untrue. It's a time to move on from old beliefs you might have once held and that have been revealed to you as false.

It is time to clear out WHAT YOU USED TO BE, in order

to make room for WHO YOU REALLY ARE—that is really what the Flowing Tide is all about, and what makes it, perhaps, the most important Tide of the year. How can you introduce anything of purity to your Spirit without removing the garbage from your life? Consider your own home. What would happen if you allowed garbage and spoiled food to pile up on your counter top and all over your kitchen? Let's say you never took the trash out to be collected and removed. Say you did that for years. Then you one day decide that it's time to do something about it, so you bring home some air freshener and spray it all over the pile of garbage in the corner. A lot of good that would do. It would just make your kitchen smell even worse. Would you then place fresh food on your counter tops that are still crawling with bacteria and who knows what else? Would you let your children play on the garbage pile?

The only solution to the problem is to completely remove the garbage from the kitchen and disinfect the entire room. Only then would it be safe for you to prepare food in the kitchen. Only then would it be safe for your children to come into the room. The same reasoning should be applied to your spiritual awareness during this time of the year. You MUST take out the garbage. You must remove it, walk away from it, and then sanitize your entire way of thinking. Start over. Brand new.

AND THERE YOU HAVE IT, THE FOUR NATURAL ENERGY TIDES
THAT MOVE AND MOTIVATE THE NATURE OF EVERYTHING ON
THIS PLANET.

The choice is yours whether you want to flow with the Tides, or to fight against them. Keep in mind however, that these four Tides are controlled by Someone much higher than any human who has ever walked this world. They are controlled by Mother Nature. These are eternal Laws and, yes, you can fight against them all you want, but you will never win the fight. All you will do is bring more difficulty and more pain into your life. There is an old and very TRUE saying: You can't fool Mother Nature. Well, if you can't fool Mother Nature you certainly can't fight HER either. Try all you want, but she will win every time.

You need to learn to accept these LAWS as a part of who you really are and learn to flow with them—to design your life around them. Do this and see if it doesn't make a big difference in all that you do.

109

How Shall You Worship?

What about Church and Religion? Your mind has been stuffed to the brim with information, but what do you do with all of the information? Where Do You Go From Here?

You've read this book and now you are wondering what to do about it. You are thinking:

> I've been in and out of churches all my life looking for the perfect one and never finding it. I now realize that there is NO perfect church. In fact, there is NO perfect religion or spiritual path on this planet at this current moment in history. So what do I do? I want to worship the REAL God, not the cultural gods of today. I want my spiritual life to be larger than my physical life. I want to see miracles in my own personal realm of existence. Am I supposed to throw out everything I have learned from other humans and just sit here twiddling my thumbs? Can you give me some advice on what I should do to achieve my own Awakening and begin to contribute something of a meaningful nature to this world, regardless of how it all ends?

God REQUIRES only TWO things from humans on a spiritual level:

- The acknowledgment of God, and
- Gratitude to God.

What follows are some basic guidelines that will make it easier for you to understand and fulfill those two requirements in your personal life without having to belong to an organized cultural religion.

THE FIVE POINTS OF A PERSONAL RELIGION

There does not need to be much detail as these points are all self-explanatory. In fact, THAT is the whole point of the Original Religion; it was a SIMPLE religion that any human could EASILY carry around in their heart and mind. No scriptures to memorize, no complicated rituals to perform, no suits and ties to wear, and no robes and funny hats. Just the bare bones of what God wants each person to do in order to fulfill a practice of worship toward God. You can't get any closer to the purest form of religion ever practiced on Earth than what you will find in the following five points. Remember, KEEP IT SIMPLE in your head, and don't complicate it.

If enough people on Earth apply these five points to their lives, perhaps the damage that has been done to the Creation Frequency can be repaired sufficiently to save this little world. It is doubtful that enough humans will put forth the effort, but as written earlier, nothing is impossible.

ONE: RECOGNIZE GOD / THE CREATOR

ACKNOWLEDGE HIS PRESENCE BY FEELING God in Nature and in your heart and in your mind—THAT is what PURE Worship really is.

TWO: KEEP YOUR WORSHIP PRIVATE AND PERSONAL

You are an Observer ONLY. Do not conform to the world. Do not be like THEM, which means do not even worship like them. Let's be honest, human culture is WRONG about just about everything, why would it be any different for human religion?

Worship privately by yourself in the Temple of You, which you carry within yourself everywhere you go.

THREE: SEEK SILENCE OFTEN

Pray in silence and listen for the answers. Silence is the perfect prayer. If you never ever speak an audible prayer again it will be just fine. Remember also that God's first language is Silence.

FOUR: NATURE IS GOD'S TRUE SCRIPTURE

Read Nature! There are no personal opinions or political agendas in Nature, only God's Own Truth. Read Nature like a book. Study the Trees and Animals. Watch the Clouds, and the Storms. Feel the warm Breezes hit your face in summer. Contemplate all that you see, hear and feel in Nature. Ask in your mind, *What is it You, God, wish for me to understand from this one moment in Your Creation?* God WILL communicate with you through Natural experiences.

FIVE: YOUR CONSCIENCE IS THE TOOL OF THE SPIRIT OF THE CREATOR

You will NEVER be able to receive TRUTH or GUIDANCE from other humans. Never. They do not have a clue. LISTEN to the Spirit of God Who will constantly feed your conscience not only words of warning and instruction, but intuitive gut feelings you can rely on. If something doesn't feel right, don't do it.

Memorize those five points. If you need to, write down five key words on a small card and carry it with you to refresh your intentions to LIVE those five points.

- Acknowledge
- Private
- Silence
- Nature
- Conscience

Carry those words with you always and pull them out when you need to remind yourself of WHO you are, and WHAT you are becoming. Read them often. Personalize them.

> I **ACKNOWLEDGE** THAT THERE IS A GOD. MY WORSHIP OF HIM IS **PRIVATE**, BY MYSELF, AND AT ALL TIMES IN **SILENCE**. I COMMUNE WITH GOD IN **NATURE**, AND I LISTEN TO MY OWN **CONSCIENCE** FOR HIS GUIDANCE IN MY LIFE.

You do not have to use those exact words, tailor make them to your own mind, but memorize the five concepts and LIVE them daily. THIS IS NOT some sort of insipid positive affirmation for you to use like a magic spell, it is merely a reminder for you to recall the Five Points of Personal Religion so that you adapt those points to your daily life. Ingrain them into your daily routine. Affirmations and/or statements of faith without ACTION are worthless wishes. Make them a part of everything you are. LIVE THEM.

110

GOING FORWARD

There is more to this world and this universe than meets the eye. Observe ALL things upon this world as well as what you can see in the deep night sky above you, as there is magic to be found everywhere. Remember that magic is nothing bizarre or of the devil, it is merely science that has not yet been explained.

Do not take anything for granted any more. Although Nature is made of Purity and Truth, humanity is not, and humans have learned to disguise Nature in lies and deception. Be very careful NOT to believe the popular politically correct lines and lies that are being mass-produced in the contemporary culture. The TRUTH is not in them, they are NOT of God.

If you seek healing, find it by turning your body and mind toward God, Mother Nature, and the unseen powers that are found everywhere. If you learn to resonate your energy frequency with the gifts of Nature, healing can be yours.

Your CREATOR seeks the Devotion found only in a single individual's heart. God hears only the praise of one person at a time, standing in a garden, sitting on a bed in a quiet bedroom, driving to work in a car. Your church is all around you, your Praise is found only in Silence, your religion is contained in Nature, your COMMUNION with God is ever-present. Remember, SILENCE is the first language of GOD.

Allow God to find you in your Silence. God is not in a building. God is up there, out there, in the deep space of the Cosmos. God will find you if you remove all worldly obstacles that separate you. God is as close to you as you allow.

111

ONE FINAL NOTE ON FREE WILL:

You may choose to believe the words of this book and to apply them to your Being, or you may choose to reject them. Free Will Choice has always governed this world, for better or worse. Just remember, THIS choice might be the most important choice you have ever made, not only for now, here in the present, but for all eternity.

Notes

Notes

Notes

Notes

Notes

Notes

Notes

50277344R00061

Made in the USA
Columbia, SC
05 February 2019